Beyond E-mail Netiquette

Setting Standard for Success

A Corporate Standards Manual

Al Borowski, MEd, CSP, PP

Pittsburgh, PA

Beyond E-mail Netiquette

A Corporate Standards Manual

Second Edition

Library of Congress Catalog Number 2002091939

ISBN 0967533538

Borowski, Al
Beyond E-mail Netiquette
A Corporate Standards Manual/by Al Borowski

For inquiries or quantity purchases of this book, contact:

Al Borowski, MEd, CSP, PP
Certified Speaking Professional
Priority Communication Skills, Inc.
P.O. Box 24505
Pittsburgh, PA 15234
Phone: 412-561-7628
Toll Free: 1-877-902-3314
Fax: 412-561-7035
E-mail: al@alborowski.com
Website: www.alborowski.com

Cover Design and Layout: Diane Holleran
DL Graphics

Foreword

Is your email box filling up? Just wait. Over 10 billion email messages worldwide are expected to be sent each day in this coming year. This exceeds the daily number of telephone calls, faxes and paper mail messages combined! However, with this explosive growth, there are many of us who are not using email to its full potential.

This is where Al Borowski's book "Beyond E-mail Netiquette" can help. It is loaded with practical ideas on how to write email messages that will be opened, read and understood. This clearly written guide has excellent examples and suggestions to improve email style and construction that will help the net novice and surfer alike.

Corbin Ball, CMP
Technology Author, Speaker, Consultant and Columnist
www.corbinball.com

Table of Contents

Chapter Four **Graphic Presentation**

Chapter Five **Mechanics**

Chapter Six **Common Sense Suggestions**

Acknowledgments

Thank you National Speakers Association for inviting me to submit a proposal to conduct a concurrent session at your Winter Workshops. The first topic I considered was a program to help people understand the need for setting standards for creating and sending e-mails.

Thank you Carol Baker Booth, Pam Calore and Lynn Fullem for another outstanding job of editing my work.

Thank you Corbin Ball, CMP, for your technical assistance and for sharing your thoughts in the **Foreword**.

I especially thank all the friends, colleagues and clients who responded to my e-mail request for their thoughts on the state of business e-mail and those who reviewed and commented on the content. I thank you and proudly include all of you in the following list.

Cindie Andrews
Mary Archey
Corbin Ball, CMP
Mina Bancroft
Brenda Besket
Julie Blauser
David Bodnar
Carol Baker Booth
Marylou Borowski
Lynn M. Broman, PHR
Lori Brown
Amy Burchfield
Pam Calore
Mark Calore
Karen Campbell
Laura Candris
Doreen L. Cary
Fawn Chang
Dana J. Ciccarelli, CMP
Amy Clark
Lois Creamer
Kristina M. Kress
Jim Kwaiser
Karen Lindburgh
Susan L. Marsh, MEd,PHR
Vincent Mautino
Lydia McDaniel
Blanche McGuire
Beverly McQuown
Martha McSweeney
Jane A. Nicolette
Jeff Nixon
Dr. Karen Overfield
Bob Padgett
Brien Palmer
Joyce Perrone
Susan Polick
Lynne Popash
Ardyce Rigg
Lynne Sciulli
Emily E. Schultheiss
Dr. Dee Dee Sharp

Acknowledgments

Gwen Davis
Sam Deep
Dawn De Pasquale
Connie Feiler
Jasmine Fiero
Greg Friedland
Brenda J. Henderson
Buddy Hobart
Jeanne Hohmann
Greg Hricenak
Brian S. Hunter
Angela. Jackson
janet jai
David Jakielo
Craig Karges,CSP
Michael Scott Karpovich, CSP
Nicole Kennedy
Juliana Shayne
Darrell L. Shipley
Patricia Shipley
Brian Sibenac
Janice R. Studt
Suzanne C. Thompson
Catherine Timmons
John Trainor
Tammi Ventura
Marianne Villella
Carl Waterhouse
Kathy Weigand
Sam Wieder
Peggy Wojcik
Janet Woodcock
Christinemarie Yanosick
Tom Yanosick, Jr.

Names in the Acknowledgment section are spelled and capitalized correctly.

Preface

To gain the most value from this booklet, you need to remember three ideas.

First, this book contains limited fancy graphics. I purposely avoided the temptation to "dress up" this publication with vivid graphics, fancy fonts and eye-appealing color. I wanted the booklet to resemble what you see when you read or scan an e-mail.

With the first printing of this manual, most e-mail programs did not allow all users to bring in graphic elements that attracted attention to the message.

You will see different font sizes, bolded text and shaded text boxes for main headings. I did this because this booklet is longer than a standard e-mail. Many who read or scan the work will not do so in one sitting.

Bolding or changing fonts and sizes offer the advantage of finding sections quickly and remembering the content more easily. As technology increases and improves, those benefits will be available in all e-mails programs.

The second point of value for you is your personal and corporate image.

When you communicate, your image is at stake. The image of the organization you work for is at stake. People form an image of you or your company by how well you communicate in person, on the phone and in writing. That now includes your e-mail messages.

Most e-mails I have received proved to me that the corporate world needed guidance in coping with a technology and a business opportunity that would dominate the marketplace.

E-mail started as a quick, informal, brief method of exchanging information. E-mail has grown to become the preferred method of communication because it is faster, less expensive and more responsive than spoken or paper exchanges.

Problems arose when people who used the Internet for informal chat sessions now found themselves using e-mail to replace business letters and internal memos.

Chat rooms follow one set of rules. Communicating with employees and customers follows a different set of rules.

Unfortunately, many people still use chat room rules that prove less effective in a business setting. Thus, organizations need **Standards** to help today's employees succeed in using an exciting, dominant and extremely useful business tool.

Final Note: You will notice that throughout this book, I used e-mail and not email. During my research, most people used the hyphenated version of the word.

My friend, Corbin Ball, CMP, in his **Foreword** to the book used "email."

I believe that "email" will eventually become the **Standard**. At least I hope it does because it may save writers time and increase productivity. Eliminating the hyphen eliminates one keystroke.

Al Borowski

Chapter One

The Basic Facts of E-mail

Three Basic Facts of E-mail

Fact Numer One

People form an image of you or your company by how well you communicate in person, on the phone and in writing. That now includes your e-mail messages.

Because e-mail has become a highly accepted, valuable and easy way of communicating, executives need to set standards for employee use of e-mail to ensure the quality and the content of documents created on their computers.

Employees need to consider more carefully the content, approach and audience for their electronic messages.

Fact Number Two

You do not "own" the e-mails you create. They belong to and are immediately available to everyone and anyone, including people outside your organization. This calls for caution, common sense and correctness.

Employees need to protect their security and maybe their careers. E-mails sent on company computers can become legal documents. Thus your reputation and your career can become open to careful scrutiny.

Fact Number Three

Most people don't read e-mails; busy business people scan or skim through e-mail.

For those reasons, you must go **Beyond E-mail Netiquette** to focus on five important aspects to achieve your e-mail objectives. These aspects are:

- Structure
- Rules of Writing
- Graphic Presentation
- Mechanics
- Common Sense Suggestions

These five elements come into play in the following two sample e-mails.

Please glance at the samples. Don't read them; don't skim them; don't scan them. Simply glance at them. Then decide which of the two samples looks more "scannable."

Example 1

Dear respected colleague,

Your experience, expectations, and opinions are important to me. I have created a one-hour presentation on how to create e-mail messages that are easy to read, understand, and remember. I hope to present this program at the National Speakers Association Winter Workshops in Hawaii and Atlanta next year. I also plan to publish a corporate handbook that offers e-mail writing guidelines and then offer one-hour teleconferencing classes on the subject for my clients. Here's where you come in. I prefer not to assume that what I have programmed into my presentation is necessarily what the business community wants or expects. I ask you to share your thoughts, ideas, frustrations, preferences, or pet peeves about e-mail messages you receive. I'm interested in how you would finish this statement: "Why don't these people learn to. . . ." Please call me; write me; fax me, or e-mail me your input. I don't know if or how I can give you credit for your contributions in my live presentations. But, I would be delighted to credit you in the corporate handbook on e-mails. If you contribute, you will receive a free copy of the handbook as my thank you. Thank you for reading this e-mail and thank you for your contributions.

PS. If your full name does not appear in your e-mail address or in your signature file, please include it so that I can properly credit you in my publications.

Example 2

Dear respected colleague,

Your experience, expectations, and opinions are important to me.

I have created a one-hour presentation on how to create e-mail messages that are easy to read, understand, and remember. I hope to present this program at the National Speakers Association Winter Workshops in Hawaii and Atlanta next year.

I also plan to publish a corporate handbook that offers e-mail writing guidelines and then offer one-hour teleconferencing classes on the subject for my clients.

Here's where you come in. I prefer not to assume that what I have programmed into my presentation is necessarily what the business community wants or expects. I ask you to share your thoughts, ideas, frustrations, preferences, or pet peeves about e-mail messages you receive.

I'm interested in how you would finish this statement: "Why don't these people learn to...."

Please call me; write me; fax me, or e-mail me your input.

I don't know if or how I can give you credit for your contributions in my live presentations. But, I would be delighted to credit you in the corporate handbook on e-mails. If you contribute, you will receive a free copy of the handbook as my thank you.

P.S. If your full name does not appear in your e-mail address or in your signature file, please include it so that I can properly credit you in my publications.

Most people tell me that ***Example 2*** is easier to read and easier to scan.

As you read this booklet, you will learn specific techniques that made ***Example 2*** easier to read and scan.

Besides the obvious visual difference of using more paragraphs in ***Example 2***, you will learn other writing and graphic tips that will help you get better results from your e-mails.

And, you will discover new insights about a valuable business tool.

Because e-mail is now an accepted and almost indispensable part of business, I recommend each company establish certain **Standards** to ensure employees understand the critical nature of the information exchanged electronically.

Some companies, organizations and agencies created standards manuals for business writing. In most instances, those manuals told employees how to format information on company letterhead.

Users, many of whom have had experience in chat rooms on the web, use e-mail as a quick, easy, informal method of transferring information.

As e-mail replaces conventional paper correspondence as a means of communicating with customers and suppliers, that e-mail needs to look and sound professional.

For that reason, we need **Standards for Success**.

Chapter Two

Structure

How you structure your information determines how easily your readers scan, understand, remember, and act on your e-mail.

This section of the manual discusses the parts of an e-mail and the function of each. It explores techniques within each part to help ensure you get the results you want and need. For ease of referral, the parts of an e-mail appear in the order we normally see them in an e-mail.

The parts we will cover are:

- **Subject Line**
- **Date**
- **From**
- **To**
- **Greeting**
- **Opening Paragraph**
- **Body**
- **Paragraphs**
- **Bullets**
- **Close**
- **Signature**
- **Attachments**

Subject Line

The **Subject Line** may be the most important part of your e-mail. **Subject Lines** should introduce the topic of your e-mail in a way that gets people to read your message.

For example, e-mails with the following **Subject Lines** would probably go unread:

- FYI
- You gotta see this!
- What do you think?
- Forward this to everyone you know
- This is interesting

Subject Lines should meet the following standards:

- Create interest
- Focus attention on a specific topic
- Stand out so that they can easily be found for future reference

Example

The **Subject Line** I used to request information and ideas for this manual read:

Help Me Create an E-mail Standards Manual

I sent an e-mail with the above **Subject Line** to 450 people, many of whom did not know me. This **Subject Line** attracted 71 professionals who responded with comments, suggestions and opinions about business-related e-mails.

The most important thing you can do for your readers is save them time. Sometimes that means spending some of your time to give them information in ways they want or need it.

To ensure your **Subject Lines** are clear, concise and appropriate, consider the following suggestions:

1. Avoid hitting the **Reply** or **Forward** button when your purpose is to ask a new question or introduce a new subject. The **Reply** and **Forward** buttons carry the old **Subject Line** and can confuse or frustrate your readers.

2. Create a new e-mail with a new **Subject Line** for a new topic or delete the original **Subject Line** and replace it with a new one. This may take you more time. However, doing so will help the readers and will increase your chances of getting better results.

   Most e-mail systems carry default settings that allow you to include the original sender's message when you hit **Reply** or **Forward**. You will see more detail about this concept in a **Special Note** in the section on **Mechanics**.

3. Avoid including copies of all previous e-mails that you have exchanged with your readers on a given topic unless you will eventu-

ally need a single document that contains every message exchanged on a given issue.

4. Summarize the main points of previous e-mails and then ask the question or give the information that is the subject of that specific e-mail.

Yes, this takes more time. But, if you expect positive results from your e-mails, you must take a positive approach. The first step in that positive approach is focusing on and respecting the needs of your readers.

Remember, if your readers don't read or scan your message with a good attitude, they won't remember your points, or, even worse, they won't respond.

Date

Most e-mail systems automatically date messages you send and receive. Do not assume this fact and do not assume the date and time are correct. This information can be off by hours, days or even years. Check your computers internal clock periodically for accuracy. You can do this by placing the cursor over the time in the bottom right corner of the task bar.

You can also check your systems internal clock by sending an e-mail to yourself to see what time and date appear in the heading.

From

The **From** designation may sound obvious. Most internal company mail automatically includes employees' names in some form.

On the other hand, the **From** designation can frustrate the recipients or limit your results.

If your e-mail address is 12345abcd@something.com, or thebigguy@topdog.com, make sure you include your name. Many e-mail systems allow you to include your name as part of your e-mail address. You do this by inserting a space after your e-mail address and typing your name in parentheses.

For example, you would use:

thebigguy@topdog.com (Al Borowski)

This is important for two reasons.

First, many people do not open or read messages from people they don't know or e-mail addresses they don't recognize.

Second, without your name, your readers have no way of knowing who you are or how to contact you in any other way than replying to your original message.

To

This should be a person or group who wants, needs or has requested specific information.

Please refer to the section on **CC**s and **BCC**s, **Forwards**, and **Reply** in the **Mechanics Section**.

Greeting

When communicating with people you know, make your e-mails personal. Use a greeting such as:

Hi Marylou,

or

Joe,

Use the person's name, followed by a comma, which is a less formal, more friendly punctuation mark.

On the other hand, if you target your message to people who do not know you, you might want to begin with a more formal greeting such as:

Mr. Bush:

Mrs. Washington:

Ms. Manners:

Professor Corey:

Dr. Jekyl:

In other words, use the person's name, followed by a colon.

I also recommend you use a **Greeting,** even if you are sending an e-mail to a Distribution List.

You might use something like:

> Hi Everyone,
>
> Dear Leadership Team,
>
> Hello all,

Important Note

> *Always skip a line after the Greeting and before the beginning of the first sentence.*
>
> *And, skip a line between your last sentence and your signature.*

Opening Paragraph - *Topic Sentence*

Your first paragraph serves as your ***Topic Sentence***. Said another way, your ***Topic Sentence*** is your first paragraph.

The **Opening Paragraph** or the ***Topic Sentence*** of any e-mail should never contain more than two sentences. If you can create a powerful ***Topic Sentence*** using one sentence, do so.

That ***Topic Sentence*** has five jobs to perform.

The ***Topic Sentence*** must:

- Introduce your subject
- Create interest
- Establish an attitude
- Narrow the scope of the topic
- Serve as an Executive Summary of your e-mail

By reading your **Subject Line** and your ***Topic Sentence***, your readers will decide if they are going to read the message, route it to someone more closely aligned with the topic or reject it as something they don't need.

For example, consider the following **Topic Sentence**.

> **I have an idea on how to make your quarterly reports to management less time-consuming and more valuable.**

Body

Using the traditional model of writing – the Opening, Body and Close – the ***Topic Sentence*** serves as the Opening to introduce the subject and create interest.

The **Body** then becomes the portion of your document where you list the details of your message.

Within the **Body**, you can improve the "scannability" of your message by following a few guidelines that relate to the three main tools for conveying your message:

Paragraphs

Bullets

Headings

Paragraphs

No paragraph should contain more than five sentences. Actually, you should strive to limit the length of your paragraphs to three sentences.

In business writing today, one-sentence paragraphs work.

Unlike academic writing, practicality should be your guide. If you can get the message across in one, clear, easily understandable sentence, don't force yourself to write two or more because of academic ghosts. Term papers focus on one audience; business e-mails target a completely different audience.

In the true spirit of e-mail conciseness, you might strive for e-mails that are only three paragraphs long. Those three paragraphs would follow the model of Opening, Body and Close.

On the other hand, as e-mail becomes the standard, accepted or requested form of business communication, even busy business people will begin expecting and accepting longer e-mails.

For example, some companies now require their sales people to send monthly activity reports via e-mail rather than conventional mail. These reports can contain significiant detail that requires more than two or three **paragraphs.**

Using e-mail to convey longer messages will rely on clear, concise and precise writing skills and using some of the techniques listed in this manual.

Bullets

Where possible, use bullets for lists of items or actions.

Bullets:

- Make scanning or skimming easier
- Focus attention on closely related ideas
- Aid in retention of key ideas

If the **Body** contains a number of points or action steps, you might consider replacing **Bullets** with Numbered Lists.

Headings

If you address multiple points in an e-mail message, use **Headings** as a visual aid. If you use **Headings**, use them as attention getting phrases rather than complete sentences. **Headings** alert the readers important items follow and serve as a "scannable" outline of the important points in the e-mail.

Always skip a line before and after a **Heading.**

Use the **Body** of the e-mail as the primary source of your information. Avoid sending attachments unless this is a standard, agreed upon and acceptable format. Please refer to **Attachments** section.

Close

The **Close** is your last chance to help your readers remember your message. Use that opportunity wisely.

End with a personal note asking them to call you about the subject of the e-mail. Or, let them know if and when you will be calling them. If you require immediate action or information, use the close as your "call for action."

"Please send me a copy of…"

"Please respond with dates and times…"

In business e-mails, the **Close** offers companies the opportunity to build good will. Remember to use the words, "Please" and Thank you."

Studies show that people read and remember a **PS** in a business letter more than any other part of a document. I recommend you try the technique. Do not to overuse the technique. If you overuse it for the same audience, you might find your readers reading only the **PS** and not the rest of your message.

PS: You can use PS with a period or a semicolon.

Signature

Assume that your readers will need to contact you for more information. Sending an e-mail without a signature file is similar to sending written correspondence on plain paper rather than letterhead.

Provide the basic information they need to contact you.

This basic information includes:

- Full name
- Address (Street, City, State, Zip)
- Telephone number and Fax number
- E-mail address (Assume readers plan to copy and paste your information into a file)
- Website

If you deal internationally, include the full address including your country.

Most e-mail systems allow you create a **Signature** file that automatically appears at the end of your message.

Be careful that your **Signature** does not offend your readers by becoming a long, overt commercial for your company or a campaign message for your favorite cause.

Attachments

Use the body of the e-mail as the primary source of information. Avoid sending **Attachments** unless this is a standard, agreed upon and acceptable format.

Many readers will not open **Attachments**, even from senders they know. One reason is that many times, the reader's software does not work with the format you may have used. What they download will not be readable.

Another reason readers will not open **Attachments** is the fear of computer viruses. Many software programs warn users not to download attachments from unknown senders.

One way to spot problems with attachments that may contain viruses is to check the extensions on the **Attachments**. Never open Attachments with ".exe," ".vbs," ".bat," or ".com" without first confirming with the sender.

See the article at **http://www.corbinball.com/articles/art-virus.htm** for more details.

Indeed, **Attachments** are useful in many instances.

Sometimes the information you wish to share with your readers is too long for an e-mail message. Or it may contain graphic elements that do not lend themselves well, or may not work on the recipient's e-mail software.

Rather than sending an **Attachment**, you may want to create the document in your word processor and then copy and paste it into the body of your e-mail.

If you do so, carefully proofread what you have pasted into the e-mail. The default margins in your word processor differ from those in most e-mail systems. Read the document as it appears in the e-mail window or print the e-mail to see what it looks like before you send it.

Another idea you might want to explore is sending the **Attachment** as well as copying and pasting. If you decide to send an attachment that includes the text of the e-mail, tell your readers if or how the attachment might differ from the text of the e-mail message.

That way, your readers can decide if the e-mail message alone will suffice or if they need to download the **Attachment**.

Chapter Three

Rules of Writing

Respondents to my e-mail survey overwhelmingly cited poor writing skills as the biggest source of e-mail problems and frustrations.

Most were amazed at the poor grammar, lack of proper punctuation and lack of clear and concise expression in many e-mails.

To get expected results from your e-mails, they must be easy to read, easy to understand, easy to remember, and easy to act upon. Your messages should be clear, concise, correct, complete, precise, and focused.

Because e-mail now plays such an important role in corporate America, your e-mails need to look, sound and read like a letter.

As such, you need to:

Focus on Your Audience

Because e-mails are electronic messages, they reside in the public and corporate domain. Almost any e-mail you send from your company computer can be retrieved at any time by any system user interested in your documents.

Thus, before you send an e-mail on a company machine, you must carefully decide whether or not it is business- related or personal. Be aware that once you send an e-mail, it becomes a legal document and can be used in a court of law.

Before you send something you think is confidential, think before you hit the "send" button.

Focusing on your audience means remembering that most people receive increasing amounts of information via e-mail. Keeping track of and remembering the content or purpose of in-coming e-mails is an impossible task. You cannot assume people remember what they said or asked for in an e-mail they sent you.

State Your Purpose

Before you create an e-mail, think through why you are writing the document. This may sound simplistic. But, think about how many e-mails you receive that confuse you because you don't know why the senders wrote to you or what they really wanted.

The first thing you need to think about is whether your purpose is business or personal.

Are you writing to:

- Ask a question
- Answer a question
- Offer information
- Confirm information
- Follow up
- Influence someone
- Acknowledge receipt of an item

The answers to those questions will determine how you write the document, how long it will be, and what priority you will give it in your busy daily schedule.

If readers know and understand your purpose, they will more likely remember your message.

Get to the Point

In my e-mail survey, one of the bigger complaints about e-mail messages was that the senders failed to get to the point soon enough, if at all. Also, too many e-mails do not stick to the point. A later discussion will show you how to get to and stick to the point.

Organize Your Thoughts

To help you state your purpose and get to and stick to the point, I recommend you start with a ***Core Dump***.

A ***Core Dump*** is a three-step process that transfers ideas from your head to paper or to the keyboard.

Many people skip this step in favor of a mental outline. I caution you against mental outlines because they can work against you. Mental outlines open the possibility that you will forget important information. That is because whatever you are writing competes with everything else going on in your business and personal life

Many of you have found yourselves in the middle of a writing assignment wondering what you were doing. That's because the brain is a multi-tasking marvel. Although you think you are focusing on the writing assignment, you are processing other chunks of data at the same time.

Let's review the three steps of a ***Core Dump***.

Step One

When you have decided the purpose of your document, quickly jot down or type as many ideas, facts, or details you feel the readers need to know, understand or act on.

Step Two

The second step involves selecting the three most important points from your list. I recommend you limit the number of points you discuss in an e-mail to no more than three.

Step Three

Finally, rank those three ideas in the order in which you wish to present them. Having these ideas in front of you will help your brain focus on them and ensure you will cover them in your document.

This step also ensures you focus your main points on what the audience wants and needs, not what you want them to know.

The ***Core Dump*** process helps organize your thoughts, focus on the main message and ensures you include important ideas.

This process takes only a few seconds, but it could improve your writing and your chances of getting results.

Use Complete Sentences

Complete sentences allow you to create a repetitive pattern that helps readers focus on and anticipate your writing style. Complete sentences, when constructed correctly, promote quick and easy skimming, scanning or reading.

The following graphic shows how that works.

Line 1. AAA aaa BBB bbb CCC ccc DDD ddd

Line 2. A6b 1d8F6 6GG Y77 nah3* &AA @3 $

Your eyes, and therefore your brain, can quickly recognize a pattern in Line 1, but would struggle to find a pattern in Line 2. The obvious reason is that Line 2 does not follow a pattern. Chances are very high that tomorrow you will remember the pattern of Line 1, but could not come close to remembering anything about Line 2.

When your writing consists of a mixture of words, phrases and numbers with only occasional sentences.

That last "sentence" illustrates why complete sentences work better.

Consider the following e-mail message.

> **Per your request,**
>
> **BOD 1292**
>
> **Seg TRV**
>
> **Initialization failed on FOJJ 3**
>
> **Sandy out Greg in temporarily**
>
> **will keep apprised**

The above approach might work well for a very narrow or specific audience. Remember though, people may need to reference this material three months or three years later. At that time, you or the readers may not remember what it meant or why you sent it.

Complete sentences and organized paragraphs help your readers remember and use the information.

Focus on the Subject-Verb-Relationship

The easiest, most effective way to ensure you use complete sentences is to focus on the **Subject-Verb-Relationship (S-V-R)**.

The **Subject-Verb-Relationship** helps you imprint clear, concise pictures in your readers' heads. The **S-V-R** creates a pattern that readers can quickly and easily recognize and allows them to more readily understand your message.

To explain the concept of the **S-V-R**, let's review a sentence.

> ***A dog bit the man.***

In that sentence, ***dog*** becomes the **subject**, ***bit*** becomes the **verb** and ***man*** shows or completes the **relationship**.

Notice that you do not get a complete picture if you say, "A dog bit."

I believe all of you created a mental picture, feeling or attitude as you read the sentence:

> ***A dog bit the man.***

Let's see if the picture, feeling, or attitude changes if we change the **S-V-R** using the same words.

> ***The man bit a dog***.

I hope you got a different picture with that sentence.

The words stayed the same; the **S-V-R** changed. ***Man*** became the subject; ***bit*** remains the verb, but ***dog*** now shows the relationship.

People think in terms of pictures. People think in terms of motion. Consider the word ***Hawaii***. When you read the word ***Hawaii***, what kind of mental pictures came to you? You did not merely focus on the word. Your mind started creating pictures.

If I said, ***A man walked down the street***, you might get one picture. But, if I said, ***Abraham Lincoln staggered down Pennsylvania Avenue***, you would get a different, and perhaps more graphic or specific picture.

Average 18 Words Per Sentence

The important word in this helpful hint is "average." That does not mean every sentence must be 18 words long.

Most business writing averages between 20 and 24 words. Technical, government, legal, or academic writing averages upwards of 28 to 30 words per sentence.

I feel confident most of you have heard the expression, "in 25 words or less..."

"In 25 words or less, tell us why we should send you to Hawaii."

Please understand the importance of this concept. Do you understand they are giving you the first seven words? "You should send me to Hawaii because..." If you take the first seven words they give you, you must then state your reason in 18 words!

Actually, in e-mail messages, I recommend aiming for a 15 words per sentence average. A 15-word average will help readers skim or scan your writing quicker and easier. And, your readers will be able to recognize a pattern and writing style more quickly and easily.

The explanations in this book averaged 14 words per sentence.

Write Clearly and Concisely

Writing clearly and concisely means avoiding "undergrad pad." Remember when you had to use big words, long sentences and unnecessary information to fill 10 pages on your term papers or 2 blue books on a college exam?

People don't have time to read two pages when one will do. Big words, long sentences, and needless information make skimming and scanning difficult.

You can eliminate "undergrad pad" very easily and quickly by eliminating the six most common errors in business writing. As you review these common errors, notice how eliminating them makes scanning a sentence easier and faster while making the thoughts clearer.

Let's review these common errors. To eliminate "undergrad pad" you should:

1. Avoid Helpless Verbs

Helpless Verbs do not show any action and make your sentences longer.

The ***Helpless Verbs*** are:

Am	Have	Make
Are	Has	Made
Is	Had	
Was		
Were	Do	Take
Be	Did	Give
Been	Done	

For example, instead of ***I am in receipt of your check,*** write **I received your check.**

In the first sentence, *am* is the ***Helpless Verb***. The word *am* helps the sentence less than you think. It shows no action.

The second sentence uses *received* as the verb. That verb shows something has happened.

Getting rid of ***Helpless Verbs*** helps you write shorter, more specific sentences. The sentence with the ***Helpless Verb*** contained seven words. The revised sentence used only four.

2. Use the Active Voice

Write in the ***Active Voice*** rather than the ***Passive***.

The key to recognizing the ***Passive Voice*** is to ask yourself, "by whom?" after the verb. Consider the following example.

The students were sent a copy of the exam.

In that sentence, *were sent* is the verb. If you asked yourself, "were sent by whom?" you would not get an answer. Perhaps that fact might be important.

You might write instead:

The teacher sent the students a copy of the exam.

Now you have given more specific information, which is important in e-mails.

Or you might write:

The students received a copy of the exam.

3. Avoid Nowhere Theres

A ***Nowhere There*** combines the word ***there*** and a ***Helpless Verb***.

Examples: There are; There is; There should be

These constructions add length but no strength to your sentences.

Consider the following sentence.

There are many things you must learn before you are promoted.

The first word of that sentence is *there*. That sentence does not tell you **where** anything is. That's why I call them ***Nowhere Theres***. They don't tell you where anything is. They force you to use a ***Helpless Verb*** and they make your sentences longer and, therefore, more difficult to skim or scan.

Eliminating the ***Nowhere There*** changes the sample above to:

You must learn many things before you are promoted.

or

You must learn many things before I promote you.

4. Drop the It Thing

The ***It Thing*** ties the word ***It*** to a ***Helpless Verb*** or the ***Passive Voice*** to make sentences longer.

Using the word ***It*** followed by a ***Helpless Verb*** becomes a problem when ***It*** does not refer to anything specific.

Check out the following examples:

It was a pleasure meeting you.

Notice the sentence starts with the word ***It*** and a ***Helpless Verb***. What does the word ***It*** refer to? We are not sure. The word ***It*** does not relate to anything.

Check out the next example.

We saw a fire truck. It was red.

In that example, the second sentence contains the word ***It*** and a ***Helpless Verb***. However, in the example, ***It*** refers to the fire truck.

In the example, ***It was a pleasure meeting you,*** we are not sure what ***It*** refers to.

What this sentence really means is:

I enjoyed meeting you.

Or, check out the following:

In a report to the company president, it was disclosed that profits were low and cost of sales was high. **(20 words)**

In that sentence, please notice the ***It thing*** hiding behind the comma. You find the word ***It*** and the ***Helpless Verb***, *was.* Actually, the sentence is in the **Passive Voice** as well.

In that sentence, you can ask the question, *was disclosed by whom?*

You can answer that question, use less words, be more specific and make the sentence more "scannable" by writing:

A report to the company president disclosed that profits were low and cost of sales was high. **(17 words)**

To get from 20 to 17 words, you eliminated the words *it*, *was* and *in* and the comma.

You can also eliminate the two ***Helpless Verbs*** *were* and *was.*

A report to the company president disclosed low profits and high cost of sales. **(14 words)**

5. Watch out for Suffering Suffixes

Watch out for words that end in *ive*, *ion*, *tion*, *ation*, *al,* or *ment.*

Suffering Suffixes generally force you to use ***Helpless Verbs*** and create longer sentences.

Check the following example.

***I am appreciative of all your hard work.* (8 words)**

This really means:

***I appreciate all your hard work.* (6 words)**

Let's try another example.

***Our manager made a recommendation that we sell the returned goods at half price.* (14 words)**

This sentence contains the ***Helpless Verb*** *made* and the word *recommendation.*

You can make this sentence more "scannable" by writing:

***Our manager recommended we sell the returned goods at half price.* (11 words)**

6. Use Short, Familiar Words

Do not use corporate e-mail as a vehicle to impress others. When you write an e-mail, use clear, simple and understandable words and phrases.

Remember, your readers skim or scan your e-mails quickly looking for important ideas.

Stay away from "consultant words" like *paradigm*, *utilize*, *conundrum*, *reiterate*, and *transpire*. Consultant words slow down your readers' brains as they try to interpret what you mean or how you are using those words.

A *paradigm* is a pattern, model or example by which you are supposed to learn something. Although *paradigm* has been popularized by consultants, many people still do not have a clear picture of what the word means. Most people understand the words "pattern," "model" and "example." Besides, be yourself and don't try to imitate someone else's words or style.

The words *use* and *utilize* do not mean the same thing. Don't use the big word, *utilize*, when a clearer, more understandable word will work. Most of the times when people use the word *utilize*, they really should use *use*.

Conundrum is the corporate word for this decade. Consultants use this word to imply a "problem." Again, most people don't know the meaning of the fancy word.

Most people use the word *reiterate* to mean to restate. If you mean *restate*, say *restate*. The word *reiterate* means to say repeatedly. Mostly people use the word *reiterate* when they really mean to use *iterate* which means to say or do again.

The dictionary tells us that the word *transpire* is considered incorrect or vulgar. Rather than telling you the actual meaning, I recommend you look it up in the dictionary.

But, you might say, "looking up a word in the dictionary wastes my time." Now you understand why you should use the shorter, more familiar, more easily understandable words when you write.

Let's compare the language of two sentences that should say the same thing.

> ***I must reiterate that nothing will transpire until we utilize our resources to shift our paradigms as a means of addressing the conundrum we face.*** **(25 long, confusing, abstract words)**

If you were talking on the telephone, you would probably say:

> ***I must emphasize that unless we find a new way to refine crude oil, we will face gas shortages.*** **(19 clear, familiar, easily understandable words)**

Use Proper Grammar

Your writing reflects you. Your writing reflects your company.

Poor grammar creeps into writing from two sources.

The first is what we heard and how we talked when growing up. Some we might have heard at home; some we picked up from friends or the entertainment field.

Consider the following sentence.

> ***I would of came even if I didn't get paid.***

That sentence should read:

I would have come even if I didn't get paid.

Phrases like "we was...," "he ain't...," she don't...," may work in the school yard, but they become a handicap at work.

The other source of poor grammar is carelessness. Most carelessness stems from a perceived lack of time. We don't take the time to critically edit what we write.

We skim or scan the document to see if our ideas come through and we quickly check our spelling.

Often, we miss errors such as the one in the following sentence.

Each of the three sentences above contain errors.

To be correct, that sentence should read:

Each of the three sentences above contains errors.

To understand why the first example is incorrect, remember the concept of the **Subject-Verb-Relationship**.

The Subject of that sentence is *Each. Each* is a singular noun, which requires the singular verb, *contains.*

The verb in the sentence follows the noun, *sentences,* which is plural.

Indeed, if *sentences* were the subject, we could use the plural verb, *contain.*

However, in that example, *sentences* is the object of the preposition, *of.*

Eliminating the prepositional phase, *of the sentences*, the sentence would read:

Each contains errors.

If we used *sentences* as the subject of a sentence, it might read:

The sentences contain errors.

Another common grammatical error occurs in agreement in number.

We will allow a complete refund to the customer if they fill out

the proper forms.

In the above sentence, the pronoun, *they*, refers to customer. To use the pronoun *they*, which is plural, you must change the singular noun *customer* to the plural, *customers*.

Improper use of pronouns causes another common grammatical error.

Consider this sentence.

Please contact myself.

That should read:

Please contact me.

To help you become aware of errors you may make in grammar, I recommend three resources.

1. Learn to use your computer's Grammar Checker to help you spot the obvious mistakes. Don't rely strictly on a Grammar Checker. It is a tool; it is not always accurate.
2. Ask your friends to critically analyze your writing for mistakes in grammar. If you do this several times, you and they will start to see common mistakes appearing in your writing. That's a good place to start improving.
3. Invest in a good reference source such as the **Gregg Reference Manual**. Keep it on or near your desk. Develop a habit of checking the accuracy of your grammar by referring to the manual.

Learn to Punctuate Properly

Complete sentences, proper grammar and proper punctuation help your reader read, follow and understand your message easily and quickly.

Proper punctuation serves as a visual aid to readers as they scan your document.

Proper punctuation is a moving target. I seriously doubt if most people remember all the rules of grammar or punctuation. However, enough business people remember some basics of punctuation, especially the use of commas.

In the last several years, I have become aware of a "comma conspiracy." Someone is stealing all the commas. Not only that, these Punctuation Pirates are dropping them where they don't belong.

To help with punctuation, I offer three suggestions. First, run your writing through your Grammar Checker. Grammar Checkers will catch most punctuation errors.

Second, invest in a reference guide to help you with punctuation. I recommend three excellent sources:

- The Gregg Reference Manual
  Order from www.alborowski.com
- The ACS Style Guide, published by the American Chemical Society
- The Publication Manual of the American Psychological Association

The third suggestion is to read your e-mail out loud. Often, doing so will help you decide if or where you might need a comma. Normally, where your mind and lungs want to take a breath, you might need a comma.

Reflect a Positive Personal and Corporate Image

Because your corporate e-mails can and may be read by people other than your intended audiences, be sure to maintain a **Positive Tone**. Do not use e-mail as a device to vent frustration with your company, bosses or peers. Your writing reflects you; your writing reflects your company. Creating work-related documents means you must present yourself and your company in a professional, intelligent and correct manner.

If dealing with customers, avoid emotionally charged "nastygrams" that reflect poorly on you and your company. Before you hit the send button on a "nastygram," go to lunch early, take a walk or ask a friend to read your document. You will be glad you did.

Use Your Spell Checker

Yes, use your spell checker on everything you write. But, be careful not to use it as your only quality check.

For example, you may use the word their, when you mean there or they're. Or you might type form when you want to type from.

Your readers scan or skim documents you write. Likewise, you skim or scan your document when checking for its content. You may recognize the great ideas you shared in your e-mail message, but you may use the the wrong spelling for words that sound alike.

Please reread the last sentence. Did you catch the word ***the*** repeated before the words *wrong spelling*? Your spell checker would probably catch that.

Use your Grammar Checker

Besides offering you helpful information about grammar, most grammar checkers offer statistical information about your writing style.

The **Options** sections of most grammar checkers allow you to set defaults that measure the length and readability of your documents. Grammar checkers can tell you the percentage of passive voice you use, the average words per sentence, the grade level you are writing on and the readability of your document.

You can use this information to improve your writing, save time and help you get better results.

Use Your Word Processor to Create Important E-mails

If your e-mail system does not offer a spell checker or grammar checker, create your important documents in your word processor. Doing so allows you to use the writing and editing tools built into your word processor. After using the word processor writing tools, you can copy the message and paste it into your e-mail.

Besides the grammar and spell checkers, your word processing software also offers other writing tools such as word counts, find and replace, document style, Thesaurus, and formatting.

Proofread! Proofread! Proofread!

Remember, your image and the company's image is at stake. Misspelled words, poor grammar, incomplete thoughts, incorrect information, or offensive material can destroy relationships you or your company have spent years cultivating.

Chapter Four

Graphic Presentation

Most readers assess an e-mail's importance and value simply by how it looks on the screen. How "scannable" the document appears sometimes determines whether or not people will invest their time reviewing your message.

Uppercase Letters

Avoid using all **Uppercase Letters** to create an e-mail. In the world of Internet correspondence, using all **Uppercase Letters** means you are shouting at the readers. This is not only rude; it is impractical.

The practical reason you should avoid all **Uppercase Letters** relates to readability. Reading, and therefore scanning or skimming, a document in all upper case letters is more difficult and takes more time.

Studies show people can read a document easier and faster if it is written in a combination of the upper and lower case:

> ***obviously i also recommend you avoid creating e-mails in all lowercase letters because people in the us might mistake us for us rather than us which stands for united states.***

I think you get my point.

If your goal is to get results with your e-mails, you should do everything possible to make your document easy and quick to read.

Font

Select a font that makes your document easy and quick to read. You can easily access a multitude of graphically different fonts in most word processing or e-mail packages.

However, you should select a font based on how easy it is to read on the screen and on paper, not on how graphically appealing the letters appear.

San serif fonts such as Arial, Verdana or Tahoma are generally cleaner and easier to read on a computer monitor.

Font Size

Standard, acceptable font size for e-mail is either 10 point or 12 point. These sizes are large enough for most people to read and small enough for the readers to capture a good portion of the e-mail message at one glance without scrolling down for more information.

Also, if readers decide to print your e-mail message, these font sizes will take less time and less paper to print.

Font sizes lower than 10 point are difficult to read both on the screen and on paper.

Most e-mail packages allow you to set a font and a size as a default.

Bold Font

Using **Bold Fonts** makes an impact if your readers use the same e-mail system. However, not all e-mail systems have the ability to include or transfer certain mechanical features from the sender's to the reader's package.

A word or phrase that appears bold in one package looks completely different in another.

Instead of seeing

> I am going to **bold** the word **bold**.

Your readers may see

> I am going to <bold> the word <bold.>

Underlining

The concept of **Underlining** started with the use of typewriters as a device to emphasize an important point.

In e-mail messages, **Underlining** may create a graphic distraction. First, the line under a word or phrase may cut off part of a letter. Someone scanning or skimming an e-mail might misread the letter and get a completely different interpretation of the meaning of the message.

Second, as mentioned above, an underlined word or phrase in one software package looks completely different in another.

Italics

As with **Bold** and **Underlining**, you should use **Italics** with the caution that, as of the printing of this manual, not all e-mail packages reproduce that graphic form correctly.

Color

Some e-mail software packages allow you to use **Color** as a background and for fonts. Also some packages automatically show your reply in blue. Unfortunately, unless the receiver uses the same program. they will receive your reply in black.

This has graphic appeal for those readers who are able to take advantage of this feature. But, it can cause problems similar to those with **Bold Font, Underlining** and **Italics.**

Also, the use of **Color** might prove a distraction for your readers who are affected by color blindness. What you thought was a technique that created positive impact might instead create the opposite reaction.

Bold Font, Underlining, and Color or larger **Fonts** create impact and draw attention on paper. Until all e-mail software sends and receives electronic messages that display all these graphic elements easily and correctly, I recommend you use e-mail for simple text messages.

Emoticons

Emoticons are graphic attempts to convey human emotion in electronic messages. You can create **Emoticons** by using keystrokes to create images that let your readers know how to interpret your exact meaning.

For example, :>) indicates a smiling happy person, while :>(implies sadness or disappointment.

Proponents of **Emoticons** suggest that expressing emotion in writing is more difficult than in person, where you are able to read a person's body language or hear the tone of her or his voice.

Some people would have you believe emotion has no place in business communication. I strongly believe emotion and feelings should be an im portant factor in business. Business people should pay more attention to employee and customer feelings and emotions. No matter what business you are in, you are in the people-to-people business.

I hope you recognize the emotion and feeling that came through in the last paragraph.

Although **Emoticons** offer a graphic expression for some readers and writers, I recommend not using them because not everyone knows what they mean.

Emoticons can convey a personal touch to your message. But if they take you longer to type and readers longer to interpret, they may work against you. If your readers know them and use them, you might be safe. Pay careful attention to e-mails you receive. Use them as a guide.

Emoticons may be appropriate in chat rooms but probably are not accepted in boardrooms. Remember that e-mail messages you send on your company's computers should focus on business not personal information.

Chapter Five

Mechanics

By **Mechanics**, I mean the capabilities or conventions built into most e-mail systems or software. Although these capabilities are available, that does not mean you must use them. Be aware of how others may use them with your e-mail messages without your knowledge or approval.

CC - Courtesy Copies

For this manual, I use **CC** and **BCC** for emphasis. Some e-mail systems use **Cc** and some use **cc** along with **Bcc** and **bcc**. Please notice what **CC** now stands for in American business writing. In the past, **CC** stood for carbon copy. Today, it means ***Courtesy Copy***.

You can use **CC** as a technique to keep other people or other departments aware of information or projects that may involve them or be of interest to them.

Some people, however, use this device to indicate a "coward's copy." They use the **CC** feature to copy their bosses or others with influence as a means of proving an action has been taken. People use the device as a veiled threat to prove they have informed others, done something or answered questions asked of them.

Also, use of the **CC** capability sometimes indicates that paranoia runs rampant in the organization. In those instances, **CC** stands for "Cover your Carcass." It means, "I don't trust you." "I don't trust me."

> **"I don't trust you to remember we changed the meeting times."**
>
> **"I don't trust me to remember I told you to change the times."**

Use the **CC** feature only when the receivers want or expect a copy of something you have sent to someone else.

To decide if you should **CC** someone or a department, I recommend a simple technique - ask them.

Before you **CC** others, ask them if they would like to be included on the distribution list. Or, when you send the first e-mail about a specific topic or project, include a note that asks them to tell you whether or not they want to receive additional information about the topic.

BCC - Blind Courtesy Copies

People use the **BCC** capability to send copies of documents to a person or a group in a fashion that does not indicate to the primary receiver that other people are receiving a copy of the document. This can be useful for distributing information to large groups who want or need shared company information.

However, some people use this feature as a form of CYA, which means, "Cover Your Anatomy."

Use this device sparingly. Be aware that when you hit the send button, anyone on the system can retrieve your document at any time.

Because of that factor, e-mail messages you thought were between you and a specific recipient, now become legal documents that can be used against you.

If you send someone a message you would not share in mixed company, you might rethink sending it at all.

Forward

This feature allows you to send the entire contents of an e-mail you received to other people. This is a useful way to share information.

It can also become a vicious method of destroying your career or reputation, or ruining your company. Allow me to explain.

People who receive your e-mails can **Forward** them to other people who can **Forward** them on to others.

You may never know this happened. Your document may contain information, language, grammar, spelling, or emotional content you may not want others to see. It might be something you would never have told anyone else other than the intended receiver.

And, you have no way to track or trace who sees your e-mails other than the intended receiver.

Use this technique only if the recipients of the **Forward** want, need or request copies of the document.

Reply

This feature allows you to send a return message directly to the person sending you an e-mail. Using **Reply** means you do not have to type in the recipient's e-mail address.

When you hit **Reply**, an e-mail message window appears on your screen that automatically includes the e-mail address of the person that sent you the original message. It appears in the **To** area of your return message. It also includes your e-mail address in the **From** area.

The **Reply** capability also automatically inserts the **Subject Line** of the original message. This can be good news; it can be bad news.

This is good news because the original sender knows the response comes as a reply to the original message.

Hitting **Reply** becomes bad news when the original recipient uses **Reply** to send another unrelated message. Some receivers archive documents by **Subject Lines**. An unrelated document with an incorrect **Subject Line** will become misfiled and either be lost to the receiver or take more time to find if needed for future use.

Special Note

Some e-mail systems allow you to set an option to include the original message when you hit **Reply**. Some systems force you to select this option as a default. Some allow you this option on the tool bar as "Reply with History."

This can be good news or bad news.

This capability, called 'threading," can be good news if the original message is short and to the point. Threading allows the person who sent the original message to know what you are replying to.

Also, if the person sends a long message with a number of questions, including the original message allows you to say "see replies below."

The most important use for including all previous messages is the need to document company business. This allows both the senders and receivers to file one completed document rather than many smaller documents related to the same subject. Keeping all the information in one document does not break the "thread" that holds all the pieces together.

Threading can become bad news when:

A. The original message is lengthy.

B. Several e-mails are exchanges on the same subject.

This means every **Reply** in the exchange of e-mails contains every message from the previous e-mails.

If all of the messages from all of the previous e-mails exchanged has little value to the message you are replying to, you might consider changing the default in your e-mail system. You can set most systems to indicate you do not want to include the original message with your reply. If you change the default to not include the original message, you can still cut and paste portions of the original message that might help the original sender.

If you are unfamiliar with the settings in your e-mail system, check with your Systems Department.

Reply to all

This feature allows multiple readers to review your response to a message someone else sent you. The "all" referred to in the designation means all the **CC**s and **BCC**s included by the author of the original e-mail.

Be very careful using this response. You may think you are responding to the original author by hitting **Reply to all**. If you intend to send information you want read only by the original author, hit **Reply**, not **Reply to all**.

If you have sensitive, confidential or controversial information that could come back to haunt you, double check the button or label you hit to send your e-mail.

As a matter of fact, if you consider the content of your e-mail that sensitive, confidential, or controversial, don't send it via e-mail. You might want to call the person on the telephone or meet face-to-face.

E-mails don't go away. Unlike paper documents that may be destroyed on a set timetable, electronic documents can be maintained or stored for indefinite periods of time.

Chapter Six

Common Sense Suggestions

Answer e-mails promptly

Answer e-mails in a timely fashion. Readers may expect a reply within 48 hours; some expect an answer in 24 hours. Likewise, some companies have response policies for internal communication.

E-mail started as a fast, easy way to communicate. Because of this, most people want or expect a reply within 48 hours.

Know when to e-mail and when not to

Before you send an e-mail, consider your purpose. Can or should your purpose be better served by a telephone call or a face-to-face conversation? I have heard repeated stories of people sending an e-mail when they could have just as easily and quickly called the person or walked to the next cubicle to discuss the information.

Sometimes complex, controversial or personal topics are better handled in person or on the telephone.

Sometimes a telephone call or a face-to-face conversation might prove to be a smart career move. Because others can retrieve your e-mails, they might use that information in ways you never intended.

Be aware that some companies print out copies of employee e-mails and insert them into employee personnel files. They may also keep an electronic register of documents that list your e-mails by topic in your personnel file.

Remember to attach the file

In the hectic, pressure cooker world of business, we have so many things to do, we sometimes lose track of what we are doing. This can result in the "OOPS e-mail." This means we tell our readers we will attach a file and forget to do so. We then must send another e-mail to include the attachment we forgot.

Also, somewhere in the body of your e-mail, let recipients know you have attached a file. Not all e-mail packages signal that something is attached and recipients might miss the fact you included an attachment.

Be aware of e-mails and discrimination

Some companies use your e-mails as a very subtle form of discrimination. Because your e-mails are corporate property, they can be used to evaluate your communication skills and communication style. This might not have been possible with paper documents because not everyone had access to everything you wrote.

The electronic format changes not only how we communicate, but also who has access to information you thought was personal.

As a rule, use the following guideline when creating or sending e-mails.

> ***Is the content of your e-mail something you would like to appear on the company bulletin board with your name listed as the author?***

If not, you might want to consider another form of communication to get your message across.

Send yourself a copy

From time to time, send yourself a copy of your e-mail message. You can check to see how clear your message came across and what the document looks like on the screen. This is particularly helpful if you have created an important document in your word processor and pasted it into the body of your e-mail.

Use auto responder messages

If you plan to be out of the office for an extended time, use the auto responder capability to inform people of your schedule. Some systems have auto responder capability; some do not. Check with your Systems Department to see if your e-mail system supports this capability. If so, you can let your e-mail contacts know that you will not be able to respond to their message as promptly as they might have wanted or needed.

Insert the recipient's e-mail address last

Unless you are responding to an e-mail, insert the recipient's e-mail address in the **To** area as the last thing you do. Doing so might prevent you from sending incomplete or incorrect messages. Accidentally hitting an unknown "hot key" or a combination of keys, or encountering system frailties sometimes respond to the system the same way as hitting the **Send** button.

This accidental action can send your e-mail rushing along its way and you might not even realize it happened.

Without an e-mail address in the **To** area, your system cannot **Send** a document. Inserting the recipient's e-mail address after you have proofread your document may help you avoid embarrassment and a lot of retyping time.

Consider e-mail "Dos" and "Do Nots"

- Do not send chain letters, indecent jokes or pornography using your organization's computer. Your job, career and reputation are at stake.
- Don't send poems, jokes, or personal correspondence on company time or on the company computers.

  Your company or organization may have a Code of Conduct or company policy that prohibits employees from using company time or computers to send such non-business entries.
- Avoid sending e-mails that in any way could be considered sexist, sexual harassment, racist, bigoted, or discriminatory.
- Avoid e-mail wars in the form of endless responses or endless "thank you's."
- Avoid using a single e-mail to accomplish multiple tasks. If you need someone to do three things, let them know that early in the message. Let them know what you need them to do, possibly why, and what deadlines both of you are working under.
- Use a "24-Hour Drawer" for documents you create when you are angry. That means you should wait 24 hours after creating the document. Then, reread it carefully and unemotionally before you send it.

Thank You

Thank you for buying and scanning my book. I hope you found it useful and refer to it often.

Technology is a moving target and what works today may not apply tomorrow. I plan to continually update this manual so that it is current and useful to you.

As you learn new ideas and techniques about e-mail technology and e-mail as a communication tool, let me know about them. I welcome your comments and your suggestions on how to improve and expand the content and value of this work. Please contact me at al@alborowski.com.

About the author

Al Borowski, MEd, CSP

Al Borowski works with companies who want their employees to communicate clearly and with business professionals who want more impact in their presentations. He helps people save time, reduce stress and get better results when they speak, write or listen. Al has trained more than 10,000 participants as a seminar leader for ***The American Management Association, Dun & Bradstreet, Penn State University, The University of Pittsburgh-Katz Graduate School of Business, and Robert Morris College.***

He brings more than twenty years of communication experience to his action-packed keynote speeches, breakout sessions, and workshops. His exciting, innovative approach draws on years of practical application as a sales manager, business development manager, and customer service manager. His background also includes four years as an English teacher. He is a published author and professional musician.

Al is a member of the National Speakers Association, where he received their highest earned designation, CSP (**Certified Speaking Professional**). He is also a Past President of The Pennsylvania Speakers Association and a past board member of the Pittsburgh Chapter of the American Society for Training and Development. He holds a Master's Degree in Adult Education and a certificate in Human Resource Development.

Contact Al at:

Al Borowski, MEd, CSP
Certified Speaking Professional
Priority Communication Skills, Inc.
P.O. Box 24505
Pittsburgh, PA 15234

Phone 412-561-7628
Toll Free 1-877-902-3314
Fax 412-561-7035
E-mail al@alborowski.com
www.alborowski.com

You can bring Al into your organization to conduct one or two-day workshops based on this book.

Or

for your next convention, conference, meeting, or retreat, you can bring Al in to deliver a keynote speech or breakout session.

For availability and topics, contact Al at:

Priority Communication Skills, Inc.
P.O. Box 24505
Pittsburgh, PA 15234
Phone: 412-561-7628
Toll Free: 1-877-902-3314
Fax: 412-561-7035
E-mail: al@alborowski.com
www.alborowski.com

Please fax me your comments on this book using the form on the other side of this page.

Comments Form

Hey Al,

You asked for comments on your book. So, here goes…

____

____

____

____

____

____

____

____

____

____

____

____

I bought your book:

- ❑ at one of your presentations
- ❑ from your website
- ❑ from an e-commerce site (which one) ____________________
- ❑ from a book store (which one) ____________________

Name __________________________ **Title** ____________

Company ____________________________________

Address ____________________________________

City ______________________ **State** ______ **Zip** ________

Phone ______________________ **Fax** ________________

E-mail address ________________ **Website** ______________

This contact information is for our records only.
We faithfully promise not to share your contact information with anyone.

Please fax this form to 412-561-7035.

Thank You.

Availability Form

Al, please send me information about:

Books

- ❑ How To Get It Right When You Write - Book Two - The Writing Process

E-Book

- ❑ Beyond E-Mail Netiquette - Setting Standards for Success
- ❑ How to Get It Right When You Write - Book One - The Editing Process
- ❑ How To Get It Right When You Write - Book Two - The Writing Process

CD's

- ❑ Beyond E-Mail Netiquette - Setting Standards for Success
- ❑ How to Get It Right When You Write - Book One - The Editing Process
- ❑ How To Get It Right When You Write - Book Two - The Writing Process

Audio Tapes

- ❑ How to Get It Right When You Write - Book One - The Editing Process
- ❑ How To Get It Right When You Write - Book Two - The Writing Process
- ❑ Beyond E-Mail Netiquette - Setting Standards for Success

Name ______________________________ **Title** ______________

Company ____

Address ____

City ____________________________ **State** ______ **Zip** ________

Phone ___________________________ **Fax** __________________

E-mail address ____________________ **Website** ______________

This contact information is for our records only.
We faithfully promise not to share your contact information with anyone.

Please fax this form to 412-561-7035.

Thank You.

ORDER FORM

Share this book with your family, friends, and co-workers.
Order multiple copies and save.

Pricing

1 - 9	copies	$12.00 US each
50 - 99	copies	$11.50 US each
100 - 499	copies	$11.00 US each
500 - 4,999	copies	$10.00 US each
5,000 - 9,999	copies	$9.50 US each
10,000 +	copies	Please call us at 1-877-902-3314

To order copies of ***Beyond E-Mail Netiquette***, please complete the form below and mail with a check, purchase order or credit card information.

SHIP TO:

Name

Title

Company

Address

City/State/Zip

Phone Fax

E-mail Address Website

BILL TO:

Name

Title

Company

Address

City/State/Zip

Phone Fax

E-mail Address Website

This contact information is for our records only.
We faithfully promise not to share your contact information with anyone.

PLEASE SHIP:

QUANTITY	PRICE EACH	TOTAL
PA sales tax 6% except Allegheny County which is 7%		
Add $1.00 for shipping and handling for single book orders and $2.00 per order of 12 books ordered		
Tax Exempt Number: ______		
	TOTAL	$

METHOD OF PAYMENT

☐ Check ☐ Money Order

☐ Visa ☐ MasterCard

Make check or money order payable to:
Priority Communication Skills, Inc.

Credit Card Number

Expiration Date

Signature

Thank You

For more information call us at 1-877-902-3314